The Hermitage Museum: The History a
and Cultur

By Charles River Editors

A. Savin's picture of the Winter Palace

About Charles River Editors

Charles River Editors is a boutique digital publishing company, specializing in bringing history back to life with educational and engaging books on a wide range of topics. Keep up to date with our new and free offerings with this 5 second sign up on our weekly mailing list, and visit Our Kindle Author Page to see other recently published Kindle titles.

We make these books for you and always want to know our readers' opinions, so we encourage you to leave reviews and look forward to publishing new and exciting titles each week.

Introduction

Leonard G.'s picture of the Hermitage

The Hermitage

"If we wait for the moment when everything, absolutely everything is ready, we shall never begin." – Ivan Turgenev, 19th century Russian novelist

Many believed that the "Tsardom of All the Russias," which originated with the rather aptly named Ivan the Terrible, had contributed to the deceleration of the nation's progress. They fared no better in the eyes of the major powers of Europe at the time, who openly dismissed them as "barbarians" that ran a "backwards" society. It was clear that Russia was hopelessly stuck in a dark ages of sorts.

That was, until a new wave of monarchs, mainly Peter the Great and Empress Catherine II, reeled the country out of the dark and troubled waters of societal and cultural decay. Fond of the cultures to the west, Peter embraced technology, science and the arts, developing a new educational system for his people and supporting a number of institutions of higher learning in Russia. He built a European-style capital at St. Petersburg and also established new ports and access to the Baltic Sea for the purposes of opening up trade with the west.

Catherine the Great came to power in the midst of the Enlightenment, which was flourishing in France and Britain, and she would rule as an Enlightened ruler. A known correspondent of Voltaire's, Catherine sought to modernize Russia and turn it into a force in its own right, creating a rich and cultured court at the same time. Over the course of nearly 35 years in power, Catherine ushered in the Russian Enlightenment and presided over a period of time known as the Golden Age of the Russian Empire.

Moreover, Catherine had an unmatched passion for the arts, and she began a private art collection that would eventually evolve into galleries upon galleries of historical treasures shipped in from all over the world. This fabled museum was none other than the Hermitage, located in the heart of Saint Petersburg, a city founded by the imperial empire's very own Peter the Great.

The Hermitage Museum: The History and Legacy of Russia's Famous Art and Culture Icon chronicles the history of the Hermitage, takes a tour of the museum, and examines the multiple key figures that molded the Hermitage into the phenomenon it has since become. Along with pictures depicting important people, places, and events, you will learn about the Hermitage like never before.

The Russian Dark Ages

"I have conquered an empire, but have not been able to conquer myself." – Peter the Great

At some point in one's life – some more than others – one fantasizes about what it would be like to be royalty. Most picture themselves decked out with a magnificent crown, luxurious robes, and bejeweled fingers, addressing the thousands of their admiring subjects from the royal balcony. With a wield of one's golden scepter, the throngs below erupt with thunderous rhapsodies of praise, which blend beautifully with the triumphant trumpets and the glittering rain of confetti.

From the moment one's eyes peel open in the crack of dawn, a band of butlers or a line of lovely ladies-in-waiting are there to cater to one's every waking need, no matter how trifling the request. The laziest of the royals were spoiled rotten, with the most indolent either unable or unwilling to dress, bathe, or feed themselves. For example, Emperor Wanli from the Ming Dynasty was said to have been so idle, concerning himself only with women, booze, and food, that towards the end of his life, he could no longer get up from his bed or move unassisted. Eventually, his negligent and reckless reign not only bankrupted the imperial treasury, but capsized the government. Like Wanli, those who daydream of such a lavish lifestyle dwell only on stupendous feasts, posh palaces, and all the glitz and glamor associated with royalty. Rarely do they take into account the tremendous responsibilities of governance, maintenance of international relations, and other momentous duties included in its job description.

On the other end of the spectrum, there were the ambitious sovereigns, who diligently studied their predecessor's political strategies inside and out, aiming to improve working policies and reform the failures. Most had the best of intentions, hoping to rule with a firm, but fair hand. With that said, it is not difficult to see how one who has lived and breathed nothing but grandiosity from the time of their birth could grow inordinately drunk with power.

Prior to Peter the Great's reign, Russia was stuck in a rut. It was, as historians described it, a dark and "barbaric" society, particularly in comparison to the major powers of Europe at the time. The period of ignorance was rife with political disorder, molded by invasion and conflict, and topped off with an identity crisis. Those blessed with the fortune to travel had seen the advancements of their neighboring countries and desperately wanted the same for their beloved home country.

For starters, pre-13th century Russia was ruled by an Eastern Slavic people known as the Rus, who had planted flags and centralized the neighboring territories around the Ukranian city of Kiev in Eastern Europe. The Rurik Dynasty, as it was known, survived for 700 years, a total of 21 generations. In 1223, an unforeseen invasion from an "unknown enemy" – the Mongols – splintered the empire. Before long, Russia had virtually become part of Asia.

Russia eventually drifted away from the Mongols' grasp towards the late 15th century. What became known as the Grand Duchy of Moscow worked to consolidate Russian territories, and slowly began to add Asian lands to their trove of territories. Halfway through the 16th century, Russia turned over another leaf when Ivan the Terrible rose to power, opening a chapter riddled with tumult and unchecked with bloodshed.

A portrait of Ivan the Terrible

The first Tsar of Russia was a vicious tyrant with a terrible temper, to say the least, but at least in his case, evil was forged out of his life's experiences. Unlike most royals, Ivan's earliest memories were far from regal and were anything but pleasant. Indeed, stability was a foreign concept to Ivan. When he lost his father, Vasily III, at the age of 3, his mother, Tsaritsa Elena Glinskaya, kept the throne warm as regent for the next 5 years. The fetching but fierce Tsaritsa defended the throne by all means. She jailed and starved one of Ivan's uncles, and had another mercilessly slaughtered. Elena had earned herself so many enemies that she, too, most likely died from poisoning in 1538, when Ivan was only 8 years old. Elena's closest acquaintance and alleged lover, the boyar (Russian nobility that ranked directly below the princes) Ivan Feodorovich Obolensky, was dragged from his home, imprisoned, and later pummeled to death by his captors.

It was said that Elena had never cared much for Ivan, but that the boy was doted upon by Obolensky's younger sister, Agrafena. Still, the untimely deaths of both parents at such a young age must have flipped Ivan's world upside down. A few days after Obolensky's death, Ivan lost the only semblance of stability in his life when Agrafena was exiled and shipped off to a faraway convent.

Before Agrafena's departure, Ivan was carefree and magnetic, showing plenty of promise with his penchant for books and learning. The boyars that took the place of Agrafena were said to have robbed Ivan of his innocence; some ignored Ivan and his handicapped brother, Yuri, while others took turns sexually abusing the helpless brothers. For days at a time, Ivan and Yuri were left with growling stomachs and their clothes filthy and unchanged. When looters charged into the palace, Ivan was tossed aside and left to protect his brother on his own as the raiders ransacked the place clean.

The emotionally disturbed boy could only unleash his frustrations on wild birds – he skewered them, wrung their necks, ripped off their feathers, punctured their eyes, and dissected them alive. In late December of 1543, 13-year-old Ivan decided he would tolerate the boyars no more. He called for the immediate arrest of his greatest tormentor, Prince Andrei Shuisky, accusing him of mismanagement of the empire. Under Ivan's instructions, the prince was thrown kicking and screaming into a pit populated by rabid hunting dogs.

Barely into his teenage years, Ivan's shell of innocence had been thoroughly hollowed, and he had embraced his infamy as a walking terror on the Moscow streets. From animal abuse, boozing, knocking over the frail and elderly, and terrorizing farmers, Ivan and his no-good friends had graduated to raping the women of the city. The bulk of Ivan's rape victims were done away with. Some were strangled either by hand or noose, and others fed to the bears or buried alive. When it came time to settle down and find himself a wife, he held a beauty pageant of sorts to choose his bride.

Curiously, Ivan was also remembered as a religious fanatic. He spent the rest of his time indoors, poring over sacred texts from the Russian Orthodox Church. Sometimes, during prayer, he drove himself into a frenzy. He screamed his prayers and sang his confessions until his throat turned raw and his lungs deflated. He banged his head against the floors, riding out the spiritual possessions until his head turned bloodied and bruised. Stories of the dysfunctional and aptly-named Ivan the Terrible gradually leaked out to the rest of Europe.

Ivan's coronation in 1547 launched the Russian Tsardom. While "morally questionable" might have been the mildest of the criticisms Ivan received regarding the tyrannical fabric of his reign, the dictatorship had its silver linings, however bleak they were. Ivan was determined to live up to the name of "Tsar," the Slavik take on the word "Caesar," and set out to conquer new lands. He succeeded in expanding the Russian empire through his trademark savage tactics, seizing Siberia, the Urals, and portions of the Volga territory. To celebrate the capture of Kazan in 1552, Ivan erected the stunning Saint Basil's Cathedral, which still stands today in the Red Square of Moscow. Both European and Asian elements were incorporated into the wooden structure, constructed with a white stone foundation and a red brick facade, and capped with "onion-shaped" tin domes painted with mesmerizing patterns in white, gold, red, blue, and green.

Accomplishments aside, Ivan's brand of leadership had more than scarred the reputation of the Tsardom. The drastic centralization of power under his reign saw the bloody persecution of many in the lower class. He established an organization dubbed the "Oprichniki," an army of rogues and former criminals dressed in black who stalked the streets with their black stallions. They were tasked with keeping the nobility in line, and did not hesitate to kill anyone who opposed Ivan. Not that there were many who dared step out of line, anyway – Ivan was supposedly armed with a glinting metal spear at all times.

The Oprichniki later branched out to "pseudo-monasticism," raising more eyebrows in the neighboring powerhouses of Europe. Together, they recited scripture during supper and performed appalling rituals, involving endless barrels of wine, wild orgies, excruciating torture, and the rape of noble and peasant women alike. These horrendous acts were followed by equally unhinged acts of remorse, which saw the sinners, Ivan included, hurling themselves head-first into walls and altars until their heads cracked, and blood streamed down their faces.

The gore that resulted from the reigns of Ivan's successors up until the mid-17th century paled very much in comparison, but the damage had been done. In Europe's eyes, Russia was an irremediable lost cause, hopelessly stuck in the past. Those who were inclined to be xenophobic disliked the Russians for the unorthodox and diverse culture that made them unique.

As the Tsars after Ivan accumulated more lands from Asia, the Russian populace blossomed with color; to some, these faces were becoming less and less "European." The Russians practiced a different version of Christianity that set them apart from the chiefly Catholic Europe, and they communicated in a different language and wrote in Cyrillic script, unlike most of Europe, which had embraced Latin. They dressed differently, donning headdresses, caftans, elaborate hats, and fur coats and boots, often in red and other eye-catching hues. Beards were free to grow untamed, and shoes were worn to bed, practices heavily frowned upon by the rest of the continent.

It seemed as if every major technological revolution and period of cultural enlightenment had skipped over Russia. Many of the inhabitants clung on tightly to tradition, and refused to accept change. This was especially evident when Ivan established Russia's first publishing house, the "Moscow Print Yard," in 1553, incurring the wrath of the scribes, as their jobs had been threatened. When protesters set the yard ablaze, the printers high-tailed it to Lithuania and set up shop there.

In spite of the Tsars' love for warfare, Russia's army and navy were both falling apart, and they could no longer hold a candle to their rival forces. Due to the plummeting morale, creativity within the country was dim and uninspired. The schooling system was in disarray, with a broken curriculum and no real standards in terms of science or mathematics.

Change needed to happen now, lest they lag any further and fall behind indefinitely.

A Glimmer of Hope

"I built St. Petersburg as a window to let in the light of Europe." – Tsar Peter I of Russia

Tsar Peter I of Russia, otherwise known to his people as "Peter the Great," came to power in this tenuous position, and though his ascension to the hallowed throne was a feat he had pined after for years, Peter knew there was no easy task ahead of him. Yet it would be this Russian royal who singlehandedly rehabilitated the crumbling nation and propelled it into the modern age.

1698 portrait of Peter the Great

Peter was born "Pyotr Alekseyevich" in Moscow, Russia, on the 9th of June in 1672. His birth was hardly a miracle to the prolific Tsar Alexis Mikhailovich, for baby Peter was his 14th child, the 1st son by his 2nd wife, Natalya Naryshkina. The Mikhailoviches belonged to the budding lineage of Russian tsardom, which originated with the nation's very first Tsar, Ivan the Terrible, in 1547.

Roughly 4 months before Peter's 4th birthday, Alexis died of a heart attack and was succeeded by his eldest surviving son, Feodor III, a bright but sickly 15-year-old. When the young Feodor died from scurvy complications in 1682, 16-year-old Ivan V and his stepbrother, Peter, ruled jointly for the next 14 years. Unlike those before him, Ivan V, nicknamed "Ivan the Ignorant," was born with severe mental and physical disabilities. He was neither fit for the crown, nor did he want the position in the first place.

It seemed, however, that the crown fit snugly on young Peter's head. The year of Feodor's death, a misinformed but malicious mob that were convinced that Ivan had been murdered, stormed into the Grand Kremlin Palace, crying for blood. A panicking Tsaritsa Nataylya promptly presented both Ivan and Peter to the crowd, assuring them her boys were completely unharmed. Legend has it, as a whimpering Ivan cowered behind his mother, an unblinking Peter, who was exceptionally tall and broad-shouldered for his age, faced the crowd with not so much as a quiver.

Portrait of Peter as a child

By the age of 27, Ivan's deteriorating health had rendered him immobilized, senile, and practically blind. 2 years later, in 1696, he died of a related illness, leaving behind 3 of 5 daughters, but no sons. It was only then that Peter became the sole ruler. Standing at a staggering height of 6'7, and the proud owner a full head of wavy, dark hair, a sweeping forehead, and a thin, manicured mustache, he was easily one of the most towering and imposing of all the Russian sovereigns – not just height-wise, but by the weight and lasting legacy of his rule. An Italian visitor to his court would later describe Peter: "Tsar Peter was tall and thin, rather than stout. His hair was thick, short, and dark brown; he had large eyes, black with long lashes, a well-shaped mouth, but the lower lip was slightly disfigured ... For his great height, his feet seemed very narrow. His head was sometimes tugged to the right by convulsions."

From the start of his reign, Peter the Great was raring to turn the ship around. The new Tsar was convinced that the best way to modernize Russia would be to emulate the customs and policies of leading European nations. To begin with, Peter, who also believed in "royal absolutism," employed himself as the puppet master of the Russian Orthodox Church, for it possessed scintillating funds separate from the state, on top of a rich supply of lands and serfs. He also strove to revamp the education system and began by introducing the School of Navigation and Maths in Moscow. The new school, established in 1701, was equipped with reputable British teachers. That same year, language schools and military training centers popped up across the nation. In the years that followed, royal funds were set aside to construct dozens of schools centered on medicine, engineering, mathematics, science, and business.

In time, Peter created Russia's first national newspaper, known as the "Vedomosti." Russian soldiers became highly educated, for Peter believed that knowledge in a wide range of fields was as crucial as the sharpening of combat skills and the enhancing of military strategies. Russian nobles were encouraged to broaden their horizons by traveling to other European cities and absorbing the enlightenment ideals of the greatest learned minds.

Young and educated Russians were now expected to shed their skins and old habits, and keep up with what was vogue in the West. At the start of the 18th century, Peter declared that all boyars, government officials, noblemen, and landowners were to retire their traditional Russian garb and update their wardrobes with stylish Hungarian caftans, French petticoats and bonnets, or German attire. Barring peasants, those who wished to enter Moscow in traditional Russian clothing were fined a tax.

Around the same time, Peter banned beards. Those who refused to comply were pinned down by Peter's men and their beards sheared off against their will. This practice was short-lived because it was condemned by Church leaders, but nonetheless, the enterprising Peter issued a yearly "beard tax" on those that chose to keep the fuzz on their chins, the fees ranging from 2 kopecks (approximately $57 cents today) for beggars, to 100 rubles ($2,879 USD) for the wealthy.

European-style architecture, gardens and other aspects of life also became stylish in Russia, with wealthy Russians being encouraged to embrace tea parties and European-style social galas. Peter shocked his own court by welcoming Russian noblewomen at social gatherings, creating a new place for wives and daughters within the lives and social circles of the nobility. Ironically, one of the women who did not care for these changes was Peter's wife Eudoxia, who was a very traditional Russian woman. While he was still traveling in Europe, he wrote home encouraging his council to suggest Eudoxia become a nun, but she refused because she didn't want to be separated from her son. Peter crafted a solution to this nettlesome issue by simply forcing her into a convent, an act that ended his troubled marriage. Once Eudoxia entered a convent, he was considered divorced and free to remarry, while their living son, Alexei, was placed into the care of his sister Natalya. Eudoxia remained in a convent or imprisoned in a fortress until her grandson, Peter II, came to power many years later.

While some of the changes upon Peter's return were superficial, others were more significant. For example, Peter instituted a new calendar in line with that of Western Europe to allow improved communication with the West. Today the Orthodox calendar remains different from the one used by the different Christian branches in Western Europe, but in Peter's time they were all on the same schedule.

Influenced by his visit to the mint in London, Peter also ordered the production of new, government-regulated coinage to stabilize the economy. Taking an anonymous suggestion from a serf (whom he later found and freed), Peter had specially printed paper created for government documents. Trade monopolies helped to fund the government treasury, beginning with a tobacco deal Peter negotiated while in London. Though tobacco had been condemned by the Orthodox Church, it was embraced by Peter's court, like so many other European customs. Additional monopolies followed, enabling the government to make significant profits as the desire for European goods grew.

Perhaps the most noteworthy of Peter's achievements was the founding of St. Petersburg, the second largest city in Russia today after Moscow. The very first cobblestone was planted on May 27, 1703. What started as barren, swampy terrain punctuated by scattered and disheveled fortifications made of brick and stone soon, grew to a vibrant, bustling city. The structure and layout of the city was mapped out by some of the most talented European architects, including Jean-Baptiste Leblond, Bartolomeo Rastrelli, and Domenico Trezzini. The distinctive buildings and bridges were styled in what is now called "Russian Baroque," the vision a collaborative effort carried out by more than 15,000 artisans and serfs.

When traveling and living abroad became a necessity in his expansion project, Peter decided to build seasonal royal residences in various Russian cities. Shortly after the first cobblestone was set in the new city of St. Petersburg, Peter commissioned the construction of a provisional single-story timber shack on the northern bank of the Neva River. While this abode was nowhere close to an eyesore, it was nowhere near being fit for a Tsar. But here, Peter stayed to better oversee the construction of the city until 1708.

2 years later, the Menshikov Palace, designed by Italian architects, Giovanni Fontana and Gottfried Schädel, was built along the Bolshaya Neva, the most prominent armlet of the river. It was the first stone building of the city, gifted to Prince Alexander Menshikov. Menshikov, or the "Serene Highness," as the people called him, was not technically a prince, nor was he of noble birth, but he climbed up the royal ladder as a statesman, ultimately becoming Peter's closest companion. The palatial mansion awed its visitors with its marble walls, fine engravings, and floors coated with laminated wooden tiles painstakingly laid down by hand.

In 1711, one of Peter's favorite architects, Trezzini, was tasked with demolishing the shack. A handsome 2-story stone palace stood in its place, complete with a spacious basement, and was soon christened the "First Winter Palace." In February of 1712, Peter exchanged vows with his blushing bride, Catherine I, in the grand hall of the palace. It was a breathtaking ceremony, set under the high, exquisitely carved ceilings and painted walls, where hundreds of guests enjoyed joyous music, a delicious banquet, and a fantastic fireworks display. 4 months later, Tezzini replaced the wooden St. Peter and Paul Church with a stone cathedral.

The First Winter Palace

Catherine I

As Peter's family continued to expand, so did his vision for the astounding Winter Palace. In 1716, German architect, Georg Johann Mattarnovi, was hired to build an extension of the structure – the Second Winter Palace. Mattarnovi designed an impressive double-winged building with matching stone towers and burnished bronze columns, featuring rows of tall, arched windows that allowed for maximum natural lighting.

2 years later, the Winter Canal was created, running from the Neva to the Moika River. This drained the land of the widening Winter Palace, and defined its borders. It was in the Second Winter Palace that Peter the Great died in February of 1725, succumbing to infections from uremia. In 1736, high-ranking court officials took up residence within the empty palace.

In the wake of Peter's death, Tsaritsa Anna Ivanovna, the daughter of Peter's stepbrother, Ivan the Ignorant, rose to the throne. The new monarch was unpopular, described as "barely literate" and unattractive, with bloated cheeks reminiscent of "Westphalian ham." In 1732, a Third Winter Palace was built for the demanding empress. Italian architects, Carlo and Francesco Rastrelli, had been put in charge of creating the 3-story beauty. Wings were later tacked on, forming a T-shaped structure, its stem just short of the Neva waters.

A portrait of the Third Winter Palace

Portraits of interior halls and the Rotunda in the palace

The small throne room in the palace

That same year, the Winter Palace complex was declared the official residence of the Russian sovereigns. As an interesting side note, the Tsaritsa may have been the real-life inspiration of Elsa from the Disney hit, *Frozen*. Anna, who never had many genuine suitors in her life, was thrilled when she finally landed a husband, and rejoiced at her dream wedding. 2 days later, Peter staged the wedding of 2 dwarfs, an extravagant affair that rivaled hers. Many say it had been Peter's not-so-great take on a cruel joke aimed at taunting Anna's appearance. To make matters worse, Peter had challenged her groom to a drinking contest, which ended with her husband dying of liver failure just 2 months later. When Peter rejected each and every one of Anna's following suitors, the princess spiraled into a state of depression and resentment, and her heart frosted over. In a spectacular show of revenge, she ordered the construction of a palace 80 feet long and 33 feet tall, carved solely out of ice, which came with complementary ice furniture and more importantly, a torture chamber.

In 1741, Peter's daughter, Elizabeth Petrovna, led a coup and swiped the crown from 1-year-old Ivan VI, and 3 years later, Francesco Rastrelli began construction of a 3rd extension to the imperial winter wonderland – the Fourth Winter Palace. He was assisted by Yury Felten, an architect born to German immigrants in Russia. The crew headed by the pair dismantled Anne's palace (its foundations were later used to serve as the west wing of the new structure that would stand in its place), and construction wrapped up 8 years later. Tsaritsa Elizabeth would die mere months before she could see the palace's completion.

By then, Catherine II, ultimately remembered as "Catherine the Great," had taken the throne. It was this progressive and ambitious Tsaritsa who would start a polished and unparalleled art collection that would one day transform the Winter Palace into the jewel of Russia – the Hermitage Museum. Indeed, the empress considered the collection so invaluable that she vowed to keep it a place of "retreat and seclusion," and she bolted the palace gates shut. To drive her point home, Catherine unabashedly declared, "Only the mice and I can admire all this!"

Catherine II of Russia by Fyodor Rokotov

Catherine & the Cultural Resurrection

"It is better to inspire a reform than to enforce it." – Catherine the Great

Catherine II was born in Prussia (now Poland) on May 2, 1729 as "Sophie Friederike Auguste." In contrast to the Tsars and Tsaritsas who ruled before her, Sophie was not a direct descendant of the Tsardom but the daughter of the prince of the small German district, Anhalt-Zerbst. While she was always comfortably fed and well-clothed, a rift developed between young Sophie and her parents, who made their preference for a baby boy no secret. Her parents fawned over her older brother, Wilhelm, for most of her early childhood, until the boy was struck with smallpox and died suddenly at the age of 12.

As Princess Johanna Elisabeth made no efforts to hide her flagrant favoritism, Sophie found a maternal figure in her governess, Mademoiselle Babette. Under Babette, along with other hand-selected private tutors, Catherine consumed European literature, and became fluent in German, Russian, and French. Her religion tutor was an army chaplain, who introduced her to the German Lutheran faith, but even at a young age, Sophie was known for questioning and pointing out supposed inconsistencies within the doctrine.

When Sophie reached her teenage years, her mother, who had grown discontent with her current living situation, decided she had found use in Sophie, after all. Sophie had swiftly grown into her looks, and had become a rather dashing young woman, with her cascading dark hair, dazzling round eyes, plump figure, and "a mouth which seemed to invite kisses." Johanna began to request for Sophie to accompany her on trips to visit royal relatives around the area in the hopes of marrying her off. Sophie readily agreed, for marriage seemed to be the perfect ticket to freedom and power, one that would allow her to finally leave her toxic relationship with her mother behind.

In 1744, 15-year-old Sophie joined her mother on a trip to Russia upon the request of Tsaritsa Elizabeth Petrovna. There, she was reintroduced to her cousin and Elizabeth's nephew, the Grand Duke Peter Fedorovich. Though he was just a year older than her, Peter was the rubber that defied her glue. Be that as it may, it was understood from the beginning that love played no importance in this union. The pair wedded a year later, and to make the marriage binding, Sophie, now a grand duchess, had to convert to the Orthodox Church, which disappointed her devout Lutheran father. On the day of her conversion, she was blessed with a new name, "Yekaterina," or in English, "Catherine."

Young Catherine soon after her arrival in Russia, by Louis Caravaque

Peter

To Johanna and Elizabeth, it was a win-win situation. Johanna would receive the florid lifestyle she sought, and the newlyweds could now produce an heir to the Russian throne. But for the Tsaritsa, things would not go according to plan – far from it. Unsurprisingly, the marriage was doomed from the get-go. Catherine had a thirst for intellect that the juvenile Peter could not quench, as he had no interest in academics whatsoever. Catherine held her image in especially high regard, whereas Peter was visibly unconcerned with his reputation. Peter neglected Catherine romantically, for he did not find her attractive, and opted to spend his time fiddling with toy soldiers instead. Likewise, Catherine found him just as unappealing, often poking fun at him and making salty remarks about his overbite and dopey, bulbous eyes. And while Catherine was poised, well-spoken, and level-headed, Peter was moody and had a short temper.

For close to 9 years, Elizabeth waited, but due to the lack of spark between the two, no heir was produced. In this case, opposites certainly did not attract. In fact, the divide between the newlyweds only deepened. Catherine's insults for her husband worsened. She was said to have constantly referred to him as "that good-for-nothing idiot" and "that drunkard from Holstein." Louise Philippe, a French ambassador and one of Catherine's closest confidantes, made a following comment about the "ill-sorted union," saying, "It seems that by some strange caprice, fate wished to give the husband pusillanimity, absurdity, the foolishness of one destined to serve, and to give his wife the spirit, courage and steadiness of purpose of a man born to rule."

Just months into their marriage, the loveless duo had each begun extramarital affairs of their own. Catherine herself was said to have had countless trysts with at least 22 male lovers, even until her golden years, when she became an obese, harshly-rouged Tsaritsa. She remained allegiant and generous to each of her lovers even after their inevitable breakups, granting them prestigious titles, vast portions of lands, and indentured servants as tokens of gratitude. Once, she was said to have gifted a former lover 1,000 serfs to thank him for the memories.

Catherine flaunted her insatiable sexual appetite, which was highly uncharacteristic of women back in the day. According to one of her lovers, Prince Grigory Potemkin, who was 10 years her junior, Catherine was on the hunt for "a viral young man...for the sake of her health." Candidates would be "tested" by her loyal ladies-in-waiting, and the Tsaritsa would then take the recommendations provided by her "experts." It became a habit to "date" more than one of her "vremenshchiki" (men of the moment) at a time. Her promiscuity later birthed rumors that she had died from injuries that resulted from forcing a horse to mount her, but historians have since discredited the myth.

Among her favorites was the man in charge of her husband's household, the charismatic and well-mannered royal chamberlain, Sergei Saltykov. Saltykov is largely thought to have been Catherine's first true love. In 1754, Tsatritsa Elizabeth's prayers were answered when Catherine finally gave birth to her firstborn, Paul, and that same year, people began to accuse Saltykov of being Paul's true father, as it was speculated that Peter was infertile. Some went as far as to say that Tsaritsa Elizabeth had not only known about the affair but actually ordered the birth. Grigory Orlov and Stanislaw Poniatowski, 2 more of Catherine's boyfriends, allegedly fathered another boy and girl that never lived past 16 months, a fact that was concealed from the public.

Catherine squirted fuel on the flames of the Salytkov rumor in her own memoir, but modern chroniclers believe that this was nothing more than an attempt to further besmirch Peter's name. 3 years after Paul's birth, Catherine and Peter produced another daughter, whom they named "Anna Petrvona."

Another way Catherine distracted herself from her failing marriage was by nurturing her brilliant mind. Apart from cavorting with her beaus, she frequented the royal libraries and read books on German, Roman, and other European literature and philosophy from cover to cover. Her political views were shaped by the ideals of Peter the Great and the works of Montesquieu, a renowned French lawyer and philosopher.

Montesquieu

The Spirit of the Laws, a treatise penned by Montesquieu, had the greatest impact on Catherine. It urged rulers to "seek a republican soul," and the author illustrated his point by outlining the ideal separation of powers after the English monarchy. Based on Montesquieu's works, which borrowed elements from John Locke's *Second Treatise of Government*, a balance in power and liberty can be accomplished through the branching out of executive, judicial, and legislative powers.

Catherine found herself particularly taken with the famous scholars of the French Enlightenment, especially Diderot and Voltaire. She even instigated a pen-pal relationship with the latter that would last for 15 years, until the time of Voltaire's death. Though they would never meet in person, their shared admiration for each other was well-documented in their letters. Voltaire addressed Catherine with flattering names, such as the "Shining Star of the North," and the "Semiramis of Russia." Another excerpt from his last letters read, "If I should die on the road, I will put on my little tomb: 'Here lies the admirer of the august Catherine.'"

These are only some of the reasons Catherine has been hailed as the "most literate ruler in Russian history." She later went on to dabble in writing as a ghostwriter, contributing to anonymously published satirical works and comedies. Even better, she was a chameleon that blended in almost seamlessly with Russian culture, and knew just how to outwardly demonstrate her new Orthodox faith.

Less than a month after Tsaritsa Elizabeth's death in 1761, Peter rose to power as Tsar Peter III. At this stage, the pair had been married for 16 years, but their resentment for another had only intensified. Peter had long developed misgivings about the union he had so heavily protested against. Some said the resentment had stemmed from one of their first public appearances as husband and wife – Catherine had humiliated him by coldly rebuffing his raised glass in front of all their guests. It soon became evident that his suspicions about Catherine were justified. Before Peter had even settled into his royal seat, Catherine's friends were warning her to hold on tight to her crown. They informed her that Peter had been openly contemplating removing Catherine from the throne and replacing her with one of his mistresses. Fearing for her safety, they insisted that the clock was ticking and pleaded with her to flee, but Catherine appeared unnerved by the revelation. Instead, she remained calm and stayed put, and as she predicted, allowed the reckless Peter to lead himself to cause his own unraveling.

On top of Peter's open display of cruelty towards his wife, which won Catherine the sympathy of the public, his promotion of pro-Prussian policies began to repel those around him. The Church was no more pleased with him, for he had confiscated their lands in one of his overreaching domestic reforms. Hardly half a year into his reign, government, ecclesiastical and military leaders alike had come to a consensus – they wanted him out. A coup was organized by Catherine and her lover at the time, Lieutenant Grigory Orlov. Their main objective was to drive Peter out of the throne, effectively seating 7-year-old Paul and Catherine as his regent. On June 28, 1672, backed by the troops marshaled by Orlov, Catherine succeeded in coaxing Peter into surrendering his crown. Peter was found strangled to death by one of the coup members a few days later. Whether or not Catherine had played a hand in his demise is still up for debate.

Orlov

As Tsaritsa, Catherine aimed to start off on the right foot with her new subjects. To show her appreciation, as well as prevent the military from rebelling against her in the future, she promoted and bestowed gifts upon those that supported her during the coup. She returned the lands previously snatched up by her husband, and mended relationships with church leaders. Catherine vowed to uphold Peter the Great's vision for Russia, and cemented her devotion to both him and her word by erecting a sightly sculpture as a tribute to him, entitled the "Bronze Horseman."

Russia finally entered a golden age that was long overdue under Catherine's reign, which has since been memorialized as the "Catherinian Era." Her most pivotal reforms revolved around education and the arts. Like Peter the Great, she wholeheartedly believed that modernizing the Russian education system with liberal European ideals was the answer to creating a "new kind of person." Catherine kick-started a campaign to design a system that ensured education for all Russians – excluding servants – ages 5-18. To her dismay, the system failed to make a powerful enough splash, but even so, she founded the Moscow Foundling Home for impoverished orphans, as well as the Smolny Institute for Noble Girls, an all-female boarding house. She also established a chain of free schools in various Russian villages.

Catherine gained more fans by becoming a vocal supporter of art, literature, and opera. In the mid-18th century, she discovered that the French government was threatening to not just censor but ban the publication of *Encylopédie*, also known as the *Systematic Dictionary of the Sciences, Arts, and Crafts*, citing its atheistic ideas and "irreligious" propaganda. Catherine seized the opportunity and invited the controversial book's authors, Denis Diderot and Jean le Rond d'Alembert, to Russia, where they were free to write and publish under the comfort of her protection.

On the other hand, Catherine was not nearly as forgiving when it came to publications that soiled her name. 3 decades later, social critic and author Alexander Radishchev published *Journey from St. Petersburg to Moscow*. Often referred to as the Russian rendition of *Uncle Tom's Cabin*, the political commentary slammed Catherine for her shortcomings, pointed out the failures of her reign, and forewarned of the potential uprisings from the serfs. Not long after the book was made public, Radishchev was shunned to Siberia.

1764 was the year Catherine began her phenomenal art collection. She struck up her first deal with Johann Ernst Gotzkowsky, who had been looking to unload the hefty assemblage of paintings he had amassed for King Frederick II of Prussia, who was no longer interested. He fished for alternative buyers, and eventually turned to the Russians when his mounting debt had caught up with him. To cover the costs of the numerous Russian grain stores he had pre-ordered and promised to purchase, the German trader offered the paintings to the crown.

Gotzkowsky

Intrigued, Catherine accepted the collection, which consisted of 225 of the 317 European (predominantly Flemish and Dutch) paintings in the original package. After some inspection, Catherine realized that the paintings were of "uneven quality," since Gotzkowsky, albeit a skilled silk merchant, lacked expertise in paintings. Nonetheless, the Tsaritsa treasured those paintings all the same.

The one-of-a-kind collection also included the brainchildren of Rembrandt, Jacob Jordaens, Paolo Veronese, Frans Hals, Rubens, and other artistic geniuses. Among the most prized masterpieces was Rembrandt's "Danaë," circa 1636. Named directly after its subject, the mother of the Greek hero, Perseus, the painting depicts Danaë in all her shapely, naked glory, sprawled out upon a slept-in 4 poster bed as she beckons for Zeus, who is seen lurking in the background, to join her.

Another was "The Idlers," painted by Jan Steen. Steen was known for his vivid depictions of Dutch life in the 17th century, specializing in portrayals of "cheerful groups in chaotic environments." The painting in question shows a couple in a cluttered opium den. A scruffy, long-haired man with a lit pipe in hand is seen with a delirious smile on his face. Next to him, his female companion is knocked out cold, slumped against a table brimming with paraphernalia.

That year, Yury Felten was rehired to construct another extension on the east wing of the Winter Palace, which was to be unveiled as the "Small Hermitage." The first of the new structures in the complex was a 2-story building made of pristine white stone, which was built with a combination of the clean-cut corners of Neoclassicism, Baroque-inspired arched windows, and Corinthian columns that lined the second tier of the structure. This would become home to Catherine's flourishing art collection, and a community of over 1,000 would reside in the Hermitage complex, mostly the Imperial family and their servants.

Between 1767 and 1769, Jean-Baptiste Vallain de la Mothe added a lovely pavilion to the Small Hermitage. The attachment came with a stateroom, or a banquet hall that served as the setting for royal festivities, elegant guest rooms, and a primitive greenhouse. Its interior was adorned with gold leaf finishes, ridged white columns, and sparkling chandeliers.

The Pavilion Hall in the Small Hermitage

The Winter Palace's northern and southern pavilions were linked by the "Hanging Garden," a second-floor walkway brimming with a maze of exotic flowers, hedges, miniature trees, and other greenery. Here, Catherine entertained a handful of guests with plays and games, but even her most trusted companions were barred entry from her display rooms.

Up until 1775, more galleries were added to accommodate Catherine's expanding collection. In due time, the Tsaritsa warmed up to the idea of visitors, but she only allowed closely-monitored viewings to a handful of approved attendees, of which were received in small doses.

By 1787, the Hermitage complex had welcomed 2 more additions. First was the Great (Old) Hermitage, which took 16 years to complete, and was erected right next to the Small Hermitage. With the new building came wider galleries, exhibition halls, and a library. As opposed to the previous structures, the Great Hermitage was more rustic in appearance, with identical windows lining the facade of both tiers. Next was the Hermitage Theater. Construction of the project was ordered 5 years prior, piloted by Italian architect, Giacomo Quarenghi. The theater was said to have been a paragon of late 18th century Russian Neoclassicism, and was spiced up with sculptures and moldings that paid homage to classical European literature. The windows of the first floor were ornamented with lion-head keystones. Statues of celebrated Greek poets and playwrights were interspersed between the gleaming arcade of columns on the upper tier.

A. Savin's picture of the Hermitage Theatre

It was just as astounding inside as it was outside. Inside the theater was a grand auditorium that harked back to the amphitheaters of Ancient Greece and Rome, with a semi-circular seating gallery comprising 6 benches. The glossy walls were made of faux marble. Classic theater masks embellished the interior colonnades, and the rest of the theater decorated with more effigies and medallions stamped with the profiles of European playwrights.

Catherine continued to diversify her collection until the end of her reign. Most of these collections had been bequeathed to the family of noted collectors, who valued profit over the premium heirlooms. In 1768, she acquired the collection of Count Karl von Cobenzl, a politician from Brussels. This package consisted of a whopping collection of 4,000 "Old Master" paintings and drawings, a term that referred to the illustrious artists of yesteryear, particularly between the 13th-17th centuries.

A year later, she purchased another collection from a recently deceased Polish-Saxon statesman, Heinrich von Brühl. This 1,600-piece assortment, which featured 1,000 unique drawings from Titian and Paolo Veronese, as well as 600 paintings from Rembrandt, Rubens, and Watteau, came with a price tag of 180,000 guilders (roughly $17.156 million USD today).

Her art collecting skills only sharpened with age. In 1772, with the help of Diderot, Catherine outbid her competitors at an art auction, successfully acquiring the collection of the French collector, Pierre Crozat.

Catherine soon segued into the collection of artifacts, finding a special fondness in jewelry. Her favorites were engraved gems and cameos, which were pieces of jewelry no bigger than the bed of a toddler's palm, with a portrait intricately carved onto the brooch. Display cases were later built, devoted to showcasing Catherine's extensive jewelry collection. Later, the Grand Duchess Maria Fyodorovna designed a cameo featuring the portrait of Catherine the Great, which has since been added to the display case.

By the time of the enlightened despot's death in mid-November of 1796, the Tsaritsa had accumulated more than 38,000 volumes of books, 14,000 Old Master paintings and drawings, 16,000 coins and medals, and 10,000 engraved gems.

The Expansion of the Hermitage and Its Collection

"In creating a work of art, the psyche or soul of the artist ascends from the earthly realm into the heavenly...Art is thus materialized dream, separated from the ordinary consciousness of waking life." – Pavel Florensky, 19th century Russian theologian

The years Catherine spent grooming her grandson, Aleksandr Pavlovich, did not go to waste. On March 23, 1801, following a violent uprising in the palace that resulted in the murder of Aleksandr's father, Paul, 12 days earlier, 24-year-old Aleksandr inherited the throne. He was known thenceforth as Tsar Alexander I of Russia.

Alexander I

Alexander believed that some damage control was in order. He immediately demanded for the Cossack armies to be retrieved from India, which was then under the dominion of the British, but while the bridge between Russia and India was repaired, the Tsar's actions angered the French military dynamo, Napoleon Bonaparte. Bonaparte had previously resolved to send his own French troops to aid the Cossacks in capturing India, as Alexander's father had initially intended. With that in mind, Alexander did not seem too bothered about Bonaparte's chagrin, for he had always taken issue with the discourteous manner the French general handled his affairs with Italian and German leaders. Fortunately, Alexander and Napoleon agreed to cast their differences aside with the "Franco-Russian Treaty," signed on October 11, 1801, which guaranteed peace between all concerned parties. And so, the peace was kept – at least for the next 11 years.

Napoleon

Ever since Napoleon's ascension to power in 1799, the fabled French conqueror emerged victorious in a series of battles, which allowed him to plant his flags on various territories across the continent. By the beginning of the 19th century, France set its sights on the Rurik empire, and after smashing successes in Europe, Napoleon started the Campagne de Russie, which translates to the "Russian Campaign." On June 24, 1812, Napoleon rallied a force of some 680,000 Grande Armée soldiers, the most "diverse European army since the Crusades." The French troops crossed the Niemen River, facing off with 200,000 of Alexander's men on the other side. Napoleon's men easily outnumbered that of Alexander's, which the French general knew would come in handy during the negotiation process. He hoped to convince the Russian Tsar into severing trading relations with the United Kingdom. If everything were to fall into place, the British would sue for peace, and Russia would agree to retreat from Poland.

As Napoleon had forecasted, his men captured the city of Vilna with ease just 3 days after setting foot on Russian soil, but that same night, the French soldiers' celebrations were disrupted by a freak storm like no other, and within minutes, Vilna found itself awash with torrents of icy rain, followed by a fatal bombardment of hail and sleet pellets that killed a number of cavalrymen and their horses. Even in the furious midst of Mother Nature's tantrum, Napoleon remained undeterred. To revive his disheartened men, he proclaimed, "I have come once and for all to finish off these barbarians of the North. The sword is now drawn. They must be pushed back into their ice, so that for the next 25 years, they no longer come to busy themselves with the affairs of civilized Europe." It seemed that regardless of all the leaps and bounds Russia had taken since Ivan the Terrible, the nation remained an outcast.

As the months wore on, Russia was thick with the seemingly impenetrable fog of artillery and cannon fire. The deserted streets were in silent shambles, with hundreds of Russian buildings either badly charred or completely torched to the ground. A buzzing noise lingered in the air, left behind from the roar of 3 cannon booms and 7 musket shots sounding off by every second. Up to 70,000 men had perished in battles at Smolensk and Borodino.

When what was left of the Grande Armée marched into Moscow on the 14th of September, bedlam had already overtaken the city. Having anticipated the impending attack, most of its inhabitants had already been evacuated. The ravenous French troops looted the homes of the rich and squandered away what little food and liquor was available. About a month later, the snow flurries and frigid winds chased away the French troops.

At this juncture, Napoleon was down to 100,000 men. Smelling a cushy win, Prussia, Austria, and Sweden stepped in to extinguish the last of the French forces. It was only after suffering a debilitating defeat at the Battle of Leipzig that Napoleon realized that the end was near. By March of 1814, Paris had been seized, and the French general had been banished to the Italian island of Elba. David Bell, a professor at Princeton University, made a fitting remark about the conclusion of Bonaparte's failed conquest of the "barbaric" icemen of the North: "Charlex XII tried it, Napoleon tried it, Hitler tried it. It never seems to work out invading Russia."

On June 9, 1815, as decided by the Final Act of the Congress of Vienna, Alexander became the first Russian king of Poland. Later that year, Alexander established the Holy Alliance, a document of mutual consent that required the rulers of Austria, Prussia, and Russia to uphold Christian principles. From that point forward, Alexander's reforms would only become more conservative, rerouting Russia to its old-fashioned, traditionalist ways.

His paranoia worsened towards the end of his reign. He repealed many of the progressive policies he had previously instituted. He cleansed foreign teachers from Russian schools and remodeled the curriculum to reflect his ultra-Orthodox and politically conservative views. Fearing retribution from former conquest rivals and revolts from his increasingly restless people, the Tsar created the first military settlements in the country, which were essentially communities of married soldiers and peasants trained in the arts of agriculture and warfare.

Though societal progress in Russia had come to a lull under the Alexander administration, Catherine's precious art collection continued to swell. Napoleon's ex-wife, Joséphine de Beauharnais, was as an avid an art collector as Catherine was. Her collection, which she had lovingly compiled during her marriage after her divorce in 1809, was housed in the Château de Malmaison. As the pair had parted on relatively amicable terms, Napoleon had allowed her to keep the mansion she so deeply adored.

Joséphine

The Château de Malmaison

The château was a little piece of paradise in its own right, with fruitful gardens, fragrant flowers, and tiny critters scurrying about. As soon as Joséphine's visitors stepped over the threshold, they were greeted by a remarkable treasury of sculptures, furniture, paintings, jewels, and other striking antiques. Included in her 400-piece collection were originals from Rembrandt, Van der Werff, Claude Lorrain, and Gabriël Metsu. Most of these masterpieces had been purchased, and the other fraction, gifts from Napoleon's conquests.

Following Napoleon's exile to Elba, Joséphine began to fret over losing her titles and property to the Russian Tsar, so when Alexander dropped by the château for a visit in May of 1814, she had prepared a little something for him, hoping that things would play out in her favor. With a twinkle in her eye, Joséphine uncupped her hands, revealing the Gonzaga Cameo nestled between her palms, which had once belonged to Pope Pius VI before it was stolen from him. Dating back to the 3rd century BCE, the sardonyx pendant was exceptionally large for its kind, featuring a twofold portrait of the Egyptian monarchs Ptolemy II and Arsinoe II, and the minuscule heads of Phobos and Medusa on the collar of her dress.

Alexander gladly accepted the cameo, but such a gift was redundant, as he never intended to take anything from her in the first place; rather, he had only been interested in befriending her. The pair became fast friends, and they continued to correspond until her abrupt death later that month. Holding true to his word, he ensured that Joséphine's descendants were well taken care of, not only allowing them to keep their titles but endowing them with ample fortunes.

A year later, Alexander purchased 38 paintings and 4 Canova sculptures from Joséphine's heirs, which amounted to a total of 940,000 francs (roughly $3.478 million USD). Soon after, he acquired another 15 paintings – this time, of Spanish origin – from Joséphine's Amsterdam collection through another third party for 100,000 guilders ($9.531 million). It was then that Russian Empire reached another cultural milestone, holding the largest Rembrandt collection in the world.

In 1820, Alexander ordered the construction of the General Staff Building. It was to be built in place of the soon-to-be demolished private homes along the Palace Square and the Moika River in St. Petersburg. Karlo Rossi, a Russian architect who learned his trade in Italy, was assigned to manage the project. Rossi's blueprints boasted an arch that would connect the new 5-story building and its 5 courtyards to the central component of the Winter Palace. This arch, designed by Stepan Pimenov and Vasily Demuth-Malinovsky, did more than just improve the aesthetics of the complex – it symbolized Russia's triumph in the war of 1812. The columns of the arch were garnished with statues of winged angels and soldiers in full gear, and on its crown, a sublime sculpture of the Goddess of Glory surfing on the Chariot of Victory.

Wolfgang Moroder's picture of the General Staff Building

The General Staff Building mingled nicely with the existing buildings, and was another standing work of art in itself. Versus the building's austere, monotone facade, its splendid interior features decorative colonnades and marvelous murals hand-painted onto the canvases of its high ceilings. When construction was completed in 1830, government officials moved in, setting up the offices of the Ministries of Finance, Foreign Affairs, and other related offices.

Alas, Alexander did not live to see the General Staff Building in its full glory, for he died of typhus on the 1st of December in 1825. Some theorized that he had finally cracked from the pressure and fled his kingdom, assuming the identity of Feodor Kuzmich, a monk-turned-saint who was later canonized by the Russian Orthodox Church. 13 days later, Regardless, Grand Duke Nicholas Fyodorovna, Catherine's 9th grandchild, rose to the throne as Tsar Nicholas I.

Tsar Nicholas I

Nicholas was given the shock of his life when he learned that he was next-in-line to the throne. He was self-aware enough to realize that he lacked both the military and political experience required for the position. Even more appalled were the Russian military generals, who were known to have knocked heads with Nicholas for his stubborn and "fault-finding" ways.

Though his constitutional reforms and fervent promotion of Russian autocracy did not sit well with his subjects, he, too, found importance in furthering the nation's lead in the cultural race. In 1829, he purchased 30 more paintings from Joséphine's daughter, Hortense. Later, Nicholas's daughter, Maria Nikolaevna, married Joséphine's nephew, Maximilian de Beauharnais, and Maximilian would inherit his share of Joséphine's collection, which included historical pieces of furniture, silver, porcelain, bronzes, and tapestries. These artifacts were then transferred to the Mariinsky Palace in St. Petersburg for a time, which Nicholas had constructed and named for his daughter, before being passed on to other homes as family heirlooms.

Tragedy fell upon the Winter Palace in December of 1837. When billows of smoke began to stream out of the ventilation system of the Fieldmarshal's Hall, the palace spilled into pandemonium. Those inside were promptly escorted out of the premises, only to be shoved aside by the firemen arriving on the scene. Despite their best efforts, the crackling flames burned on for 3 more days before it was finally quelled. While almost all the displays had been recovered, mostly unscathed, including the imperial throne, guards banners, and paintings from the Military Gallery, the palace interior was destroyed. Even worse, 30 guards were said to have lost their lives in the fire.

The throne room

Vasily Stasov and Alexander Briullov were tasked with rebuilding the marred sections of the palace facade and parade halls, and its interior, respectively. By 1839, the palace makeover had resulted in flame-resistant stone and brick walls, and brand-new staircases fashioned out of stone and cast-iron. The Jordan Staircase in the Fieldmarshal's Room, a white marble beauty perched upon a trio of arches, was among the pair's most praised restorations. The room housing the so-called "imperial staircase" featured divided flights dressed in royal-red carpeting, bronze chandeliers, more gold leaf embellishments, and a mural of Olympian gods painted across the expanse of the ceiling.

The Armorial Hall, spanning 1,000 square meters in size, was also redesigned. Made to hold royal ceremonies, Stasov installed sleek wooden floors, jewel-encrusted chandeliers, gilded flute columns, and life-sized statues, and the walls given a new lick of white paint. In total, the renovations amounted to 100,000 rubles ($2.879 million USD).

Between 1840 and 1843, Stasov was re-employed to begin another round of renovations in the Southern Pavilion of the palace. Meanwhile, the German architect, Leo von Klenze, was put in charge of constructing a new building specifically engineered to both store displays and accommodate the guests of a public museum. The project, known as the "New Hermitage," was overseen by Stasov and Nikolai Yefimov. A stately portico served as the entrance to the new building, supported by square columns and majestic granite sculptures of strapping men holding up the roof, or as it is known in the architectural world – "Atlantes."

The New Hermitage

Klenze announced the completion of the New Hermitage in 1851. The year before, Nicholas had procured another collection from Cristoforo Barbarigo in Venice, which included 5 new paintings from Titian, all in mint condition. Among the cherished oil paintings was "The Penitent Mary Magdalene." The biblical maiden is seen looking up to the skies with a hand pressed against her heart and her dress drooping down one side of her shoulder, eyes brimming with remorse and lips ajar in her daze.

On February 5, 1852, the New Hermitage opened its doors for public viewing for the very first time. The grand opening lived up to its name indeed, attracting hundreds who impatiently queued up for a tour. Following the likes of a ribbon-cutting ceremony, the festivities continued to the Hermitage Theatre, where esteemed guests were treated to a concert and play, followed by a banquet for 600 in the Skylight Halls. That year, the Egyptian exhibit was established, furnished largely by artifacts provided by Maximilian, the Tsar's son-in-law.

To boost security measures, Nicholas issued the "Guidelines on Management of the Imperial Heritage," which was published a year before the museum opening. In this manifesto was a carefully diagrammed staff list, the rules for admission, and even tips on maximizing the museum's exposure. In 1863, employees were refreshed with new faces; the museum also appointed its first director, S. L. Gedeonov. 3 years later, Gedeonov decided to eliminate entrance fees altogether. This risky move soon proved to have paid off, for admission rates skyrocketed. By 1880, the New Hermitage was receiving at least 50,000 unique guests annually.

Repurposed

"It is better to abolish serfdom from above than to wait for it to abolish itself from below." – Tsar Alexander II, 1856 speech

In early March of 1855, just 3 years after the opening of the New Hermitage, Tsar Nicholas I died from pneumonia complications. Later that day, his son, Alexander Romanov, was elected to succeed him, and in August of that year, was crowned in Moscow as Tsar Alexander II. Though Alexander had received the crown amidst the turmoil of the Crimean War, he was determined to fight for peace and freedom for the people of his empire. He condemned the war he never started right off the bat, and he fought to stamp out the flames of conflict before it could spread. A year later, the war was finally nipped in the bud with the 1856 Treaty of Paris.

Alexander II in the Winter Palace

Russia may have lost the war, but the wings of the empire would only spread further under Alexander's reign. He succeeded in adding new territories in the Caucasus, as well as Central and East Asia, to his empire, and paved a new path for Russia with his multiple reforms. The year the Crimean War drew to a close, Alexander founded a special committee that would cater to the "Consideration of the Conditions of the Peasants." A year later, military settlements were terminated.

Alexander made it his goal to introduce a reformative charter every year. He went on to introduce methods of budget transparency, trial by jury, and universal conscription, and called for the abolishment of corporal punishment. Moreover, he created a refined credit and banking system, and instituted new policies that allowed independent companies and merchants to thrive. He would also play a hand in broadening the freedoms of the university and press.

The most powerful of Alexander's reforms would come with a charter published in March of 1861, known as the "Emancipation Act." Like his father, Alexander had always been an outspoken critic of the antiquated serfdom system, which bound the enslaved Russian serfs to their landlords. Having established that, Russian serfs, which made up over a third of the population, differed from traditional American slaves; American slaves were regarded as "disposable" possessions that personally belonged to their masters, whereas serfs were required to submit to the landlords so long as they lived on their land.

The Emancipation Manifesto came with 17 legislative acts, or as they were known as a whole, "Regulations Concerning Peasants Leaving Serf Dependence." Not only did the charter call for the liberation of serfs in both household and private estates, they were honored the full rights of free citizens. They could now purchase their own plots of land and businesses, and tie the knot as they pleased, without the previously required consent of their landlords or other authority figures.

1861 was a year blessed in more ways than one. Towards the end of the year, the director of the Hermitage, Stepan Gedeonov, completed another large order with the papal government in the Vatican. The Marquis Giampietro Campana Collection, assembled by the Roman president of the Monte di Pieta Bank, came with a scandalous tale of origin. As the story goes, Campana, another art enthusiast, allowed his part-time hobby to consume him. The moment it was discovered that the banker had been embezzling funds to power his passion, it all came crashing down on him. Campana's properties were swiftly snatched up by the government. The banker was then sentenced to 20 years of hard labor, but due to the outpouring of sympathy from the public, he was exiled instead. To settle Campana's debts, the papacy auctioned off his prized collection. In total, the Hermitage acquired 500 vases, 200 bronze sculptures, and hundreds of marble statues from the Campana catalog. Included was a king-sized statue of the Roman god Jupiter, as well as the 9 Muses of Greece, the Regina Vasorum, a centuries-old Cumaen clay vase outfitted with gold leaf, black lacquer, and individually crafted figures of the Eleusinian gods.

More collections and art pieces were added to the multiplying exhibits over the years. 4 years later, Alexander purchased the "Madonna Litta," allegedly a Leonardo da Vinci original, which depicted the Blessed Mother breastfeeding Baby Jesus. In 1870, Gedeonov purchased another painting with a similar theme – Raphael's "Madonna and the Child." This tempera painting, which showed Mary balancing the baby in one hand, and an open book with the other, cost 310,000 francs ($1.15 million USD).

Following the assassination of Alexander II in 1881, the Russian crown was passed down to his son, Alexander III, but the Hermitage expansion chugged steadily along, continuing well on into the 20th century. In 1884, Alexander III secured the A. P. Basilewski Collection for 6 million francs ($22.2 million USD). Over the 4 decades he spent in Paris, the Russian diplomat had built a treasury of wonders from Renaissance and Medieval Europe, which included Byzantine, Christian, Gothic, and Romanesque artifacts from the 12th-16th centuries. A year later, the Imperial Tsarskoye Selo Arsenal Collection, which featured Russian and Asian tools, arms, and armor, was transferred to the Hermitage.

In November of 1894, the son of Alexander III, Nikolay Alexandrovich Romanov, replaced his father at the throne as Tsar Nicholas II. A decade later, Nicholas ordered the eviction of all the residents at the Winter Palace, while the imperial residence was formally relocated to the Alexander Palace in the town of Tsarskoye Selo, St. Petersburg. Henceforth, the Winter Palace was only to be used for official ceremonies.

In 1912, Maria Benois, the wife of a local architect, decided to sell a Leonardo da Vinci piece she had been gifted by her father. The painting, simply entitled "Madonna and the Child," another take on the Virgin Mary and her son, showed the haloed pair playing gleefully, with the chubby baby sitting up on his mother's lap. A buyer from London had offered Benois 500,000 francs ($1.85 million USD) for the painting, but when she heard that the Hermitage was struggling to raise funds to surpass their competitors, she decided to part with the heirloom at a discounted price as a "gesture of goodwill." 2 years later, the Hermitage purchased the piece for 150,000 rubles.

On October 10, 1915, a year following the outbreak of World War I, the Winter Palace was converted to a hospital, which was to be used by the Red Cross. All the state rooms, with the exception of St. George's Hall, were temporarily remodeled to fit the requirements of the makeshift healing center. The rooms were packed with enough beds, surgical facilities, and medical equipment to tend 1,000 patients, funded by Tsar Nicholas II. The Red Cross was responsible for organizing the medical crew at the palace, which consisted of a chief doctor, 120 orderlies, 50 nurses, 34 surgeons, 26 supplementary staff, and 10 paper-pushers to handle all the paperwork. In addition to that, there was another part-time team made up of oculists, throat doctors, larynx specialists, and therapists. The soldiers' wing in the palace was said to have been the most advanced in the hospital, as it utilized the most innovative – and at times, untested – surgical and medical techniques of the period.

The hospital ward

On October 27, 1917, opposing forces barged into the palace. As rival troops wreaked havoc within the hospital, the staff scrambled to gather the patients and usher them out to safety. When the invaders finally cleared out of the palace by the end of the day, the rest of the patients were transferred to nearby hospitals. With the palace gates damaged and the security of the vulnerable patients and staff compromised, the hospital closed its doors 11 days later.

That year, Russia was battered by 2 revolutions. The first, known as the February Revolution, saw mass demonstrations that lasted for 8 days. Protesters decried the oppressive regime of the autocratic monarch, the deplorable working conditions of city workers, and the abhorrent treatment of peasants, upon a myriad of other grievances. The rebellious forces of the Russian Army decided to ally themselves with the demonstrators, which led to the forced resignation of the Russian sovereign. On March 15, 1917, Tsar Nicholas II surrendered his crown. Not only had Nicholas closed the curtains on the Romanov Dynasty, he would go down in history as Russia's very last emperor.

Following the October Uprising, otherwise known as the "Bolshevik Revolution," the Winter Palace and the Imperial Hermitage were officially declared state museums, and unified as one.

Perpetual Preservation

"The skeleton is still imperial, even if much of the skin is missing." – John Gunther, Inside Russia Today, 1962

When the First World War came to an end, private art collections across the nation were divvied up and distributed among the state museums. This meant that the Hermitage exhibits only continued to grow, welcoming new shipments of historical spectacles from the Alexander, Catherine, Stroganov, and Yusupov Palaces. It was at this point that the Russian people began to feel the gravity of just how paramount the irreplaceable collections of the Hermitage truly were.

In 1922, a series of 17th-19th century paintings from the Kushelevskaya Gallery of the Academy of Fine Arts was transferred to the Hermitage. Included was Jacob Jordaens' "Bean King," which features the festival of the 3 Magi. The "Bean King" is seen seated in the center of the scene, his face slack from his inebriation and a glass goblet in his hand. Judging by the half-eaten pie in front of him, he has won the game. His "court," which includes a queen, a chamberlain, jester, cook, musician, and more, is seen pictured around him, cheering him on.

Another in this stirring collection was the "Angel of the Death," painted by French artist Horace Vernet. This haunting, but delicate piece shows a fair maiden with flowing golden locks and a white nightgown, held in the embrace of the angel of death. Death sports a hooded black robe and a matching pair of wings, but absent is the hokey scythe, which was typical for the Grim Reaper-type character that was most popular with artists during the time. The dying maiden's eyes are sealed shut, her expression the picture of serenity. The other young man depicted, presumably the love of her life, exhibits contradictory emotions as he kneels down by the foot of the bed, his head bowed in urgent prayer.

That fateful year dog-eared yet another page in Russian history. On December 30, 1922, the Union of Soviet Socialist Republics (USSR) was established. Otherwise known as the Soviet Union, the formidable communist empire declared absolute authority over the territories of Russia, Ukraine, Belorussia, and the Transcaucasian Federation – namely, Georgia, Armenia, and Azerbaijan. It became the first of its kind to base their policies solely on the principles of

Marxist socialism. Russia, along with the rest of the USSR, was now a one-party socialist state, under the governance of the Russian Communist Party, founded by Vladimir Lenin. In 1922, Joseph Stalin was installed as the General Secretary of the wordily-named Central Committee of the Communist Party of the Soviet Union, a post that has been described as "synonymous with the 'Leader of the Soviet Union.'" In the decades that followed, the USSR expansion continued to evolve, wrapping its tentacles around 15 republics in total. Uzbekistan, Estonia, Moldova, Kazakhstan, Kyrgyzstan, Turkmenistan, Tajikistan, Latvia, and Lithuania, were later added to the empire's territories.

At this stage, Russia had joined the rest of Europe, and it was at the prime of the 20th century Industrial Age. As time would tell, this was a double-edged sword, as the nation labored to keep up with the demands of the rapid widespread industrialization. This was a principal facet of Stalin's first version of the Soviet Union's "5 Year Plan." It was a last resort of sorts, as Stalin had already ordered for the seizure of furniture, jewelry, art collection, and other valuables and property from both the Church and Russian nobility.

In February of 1928, both the State Russian Museum and the Imperial Hermitage were tasked with compiling a list of paintings, artifacts, and other artworks they were willing to cough up for the sake of a "better Russia." Each list was to amount to 2 million rubles, and its profits to be handed over to the state. To ensure smooth transactions and maximum efficiency, the "Antiquariat" was established to supervise all exchanges and advise the directors of the museum boards. With time running against them, Stalin hastened to accelerate the sales, demanding that the museums move their products, pronto. All in all, the Hermitage was made to shell out approximately 250 paintings for, at the very least, 5,000 rubles a pop.

The first international offer came from Calouste Gulbenkian, a wealthy Armenian businessman based in Britain, most famed for the founding of the Iraq Petroleum Company. Gulbenkian declined to pay cash for the first Hermitage pieces he acquired, electing instead, to pay with petroleum. This soon irritated the museum director, who proceeded to drop Gulbenkian.

The dreadful sale, which went live in around 1932, has been described as "the most difficult period in the history of the Hermitage Museum." Those at the museum were physically pained to see the priceless masterpieces, no matter the size, go at practically criminally low prices. Even more cringe-inducing, officials from the Commisariat of Foreign Trade were said to have taken paintings, sculptures, artifacts – at times, even entire collections – willy-nilly and presented them as gifts to government officials and foreign allies. Those who were "friends of the Soviet Union," also received – as those at the Hermitage believed – an undeserving discount.

Many of the staff were said to have done all they could to decelerate the sales. Some spoke ill of the art, and others talked down the pieces potential customers were eyeing in the hopes of thwarting a sale. There were even those that peeled paintings off the displays and plucked artifacts from pedestals, stowing them away for safekeeping.

Throughout the extent of the Hermitage Sale, Joseph Orbeli, who would soon become the new director of the Hermitage, drew up a series of letters that criticized the sale of the museum art, likening it to the decay of Russian culture. In 1934, Stalin finally agreed to call off the sale. By then, 2,880 paintings within the Hermitage had already been sent abroad. 250 of the departed pieces were classified as major works from Old Masters, and another 50 as "world masterpieces." While the museum managed to retrieve a portion of what was lost in the following decades, 48 of the world masterpieces were gone for good. Among the permanently missing were original pieces from Titian, Watteau, and Rembrandt, as well as several pieces in the Scythian Gold Collection.

On December 25, 1991, the rippling crimson-and-gold flag of the Soviet Union was flown over the Kremlin for what would be the very last time. A few days earlier, a summit had been held in the city of Alma-Ata (now Almaty) in Kazakhstan, with representatives from 11 of the USSR republics in attendance. There, they intimated their collective decision to pull out of the Soviet Union. At long last, the Soviet Union was no more. That same day, the disillusioned Soviet President, Mikhail Gorbachev, tendered his resignation. And that was the long-awaited end of the frightening, and often gruesome era.

The new Parliament of the Russian Federation issued a law that banned the sale of national art treasures abroad. Authorities at the Hermitage worked to patch up their rocky relationships with other museums, and smooth over the tense, competitive nature the industry naturally spawned. Mikhail Piotrovsky, the director of the Hermitage, encouraged a kind of lending program that local and foreign museums were to take part in. In the years that followed, the National Gallery of Art in Washington, D.C., would become one of the most enthusiastic partakers of the program. They exchanged a number of their paintings with the Russian museum, including a few that had been purchased by American banker, Andrew Mellon, during the Hermitage Sale.

Today, the Hermitage Museum in St. Petersburg remains high on the list of the largest art museums in the world. The museum encompasses 6 buildings along the Neva River – its main complex, the blue-and-white marvel that is the Winter Palace; the Menshikov Palace, the Storage Facility at Staraya Derevnya, and the eastern block of the General Staff Building. It holds over 3 million individual treasures and counting, dating from as far back as the Stone Age to contemporary pieces from the 20th century. 120 rooms within the museum alone are dedicated to Western European art, displaying the works of Vincent van Gogh, Picasso, Tiepolo, and other prodigies of the art world.

The Hermitage family has also since expanded. Other than hosting more than 70 resident cats, the museum is now linked to 8 sister galleries, including the Hermitage Amsterdam, Hermitage Barcelona, Ermitage Italia, the Guggenheim Hermitage Museum in the Lithuanian capital of Vilnius, and more. As to be expected, the Hermitage remains the most frequented tourist spot in all of Russia. In 2016, the museum broke a new record when it clocked a total of 3,688,031 visitors, surpassing the previous year by over 300,000.

Needless to say, it comes as no surprise that those numbers continue to climb to this day.

Online Resources

Other books about Russian history by Charles River Editors

Other books about the Hermitage on Amazon

Further Reading

Authors, The State Hermitage Museum. "Hermitage in Facts and Figures." *The State Hermitage Museum*. The State Hermitage Museum, 2007. Web. 1 May 2017. <https://www.hermitagemuseum.org/wps/portal/hermitage/about/facts_and_figures>.

Authors, Saint Petersburg . "The Winter Palace." *Saint Petersburg* . Saint Petersburg.Com, 2014. Web. 1 May 2017. <http://www.saint-petersburg.com/palaces/winter-palace/>.

Editors, Castles and Palaces of the World. "Winter Palace (Zimni Dvorets)." *Every Castle - Castles and Palaces of the World*. Every Castle, Ltd., 2015. Web. 1 May 2017. <http://www.everycastle.com/Winter-Palace.html>.

Siegal, Nina. "A Hermitage Amsterdam Show Looks Closer at Catherine the Great." *The New York Times*. The New York Times Company, 8 Sept. 2016. Web. 1 May 2017. <https://www.nytimes.com/2016/09/08/arts/international/a-hermitage-amsterdam-show-looks-closer-at-catherine-the-great.html?_r=0>.

Editors, Biography.Com. "Catherine II." *Biography.Com*. A&E Television Networks, LLC, 28 Apr. 2017. Web. 1 May 2017. <http://www.biography.com/people/catherine-ii-9241622>.

Editors, Russiapedia. "Prominent Russians: Catherine II the Great." *Russiapedia*. Autonomous Nonprofit Organization, 2005. Web. 1 May 2017. <http://russiapedia.rt.com/prominent-russians/the-romanov-dynasty/catherine-ii-the-great/>.

Editors, Boundless. "Catherine's Domestic Policies." *Boundless*. Boundless, Ltd., 21 Nov. 2016. Web. 1 May 2017. <https://www.boundless.com/world-history/textbooks/boundless-world-history-textbook/enlightened-despots-1110/catherine-the-great-and-russia-1115/catherine-s-domestic-policies-1135-17717/>.

Authors, The State Hermitage Museum. "Sale of Works of Art and Transfer of Art Objects to Museums of Union Republics." *The State Hermitage Museum*. The State Hermitage Museum, 2017. Web. 1 May 2017.

<https://www.hermitagemuseum.org/wps/portal/hermitage/explore/history/historical-article/1900/sale/?lng=>.

C, Davide. "The History of St Petersburg." *St Petersburg Essential Guide*. St Petersburg Essential Guide.Com, 2015. Web. 1 May 2017. <http://www.st-petersburg-essentialguide.com/history-of-st-petersburg.html#BEFORE-PETER-THE-GREAT>.

Cheney, Ian. "How Peter the Great Modernized Russia." *Construction Literature Magazine*. Construction Literature Magazine, Inc., 2013. Web. 1 May 2017. <http://constructionlitmag.com/culture/how-peter-the-great-modernized-russia/>.

Editors, Epic World History. "Wanli - Ming Dynasty Emperor." *Epic World History*. Blogger, 2012. Web. 1 May 2017. <http://epicworldhistory.blogspot.tw/2012/04/wanli-ming-dynasty-emperor.html>.

Editors, Biography.Com. "Peter the Great." *Biography.Com*. A&E Television Networks, LLC, 28 Apr. 2017. Web. 1 May 2017. <http://www.biography.com/people/peter-the-great-9542228>.

Bos, Joan. "Ivan V of Russia." *Mad Monarchs*. Mad Monarchs, Ltd., 12 Sept. 2011. Web. 1 May 2017. <http://madmonarchs.guusbeltman.nl/madmonarchs/ivan5/ivan5_bio.htm>.

Bos, Joan. "Ivan IV of Russia." *Mad Monarchs*. Mad Monarchs, Ltd., 12 Sept. 2011. Web. 1 May 2017. <http://madmonarchs.guusbeltman.nl/madmonarchs/ivan4/ivan4_bio.htm>.

Editors, Reference.Com. "What were the accomplishments of Ivan the Terrible?" *Reference.Com*. IAC Publishing, LLC, 2014. Web. 1 May 2017. <https://www.reference.com/history/were-accomplishments-ivan-terrible-51f4ba5d6fb2de76>.

Editors, Sacred Destination. "St. Basil's Cathedral." *Sacred Destination*. Sacred Destination, Ltd., 2010. Web. 1 May 2017. <http://www.sacred-destinations.com/russia/moscow-st-basil-cathedral>.

Editors, To Discover Russia. "TRADITIONAL RUSSIAN CLOTHING." *To Discover Russia*. To Discover Russia, Ltd., 2013. Web. 1 May 2017. <http://todiscoverrussia.com/traditional-russian-clothing/>.

Trueman, C. N. "Peter the Great – Domestic Reforms." *The History Learning Site*. The History Learning Site, Ltd., 28 May 2015. Web. 2 May 2017. <http://www.historylearningsite.co.uk/peter-the-great/peter-the-great-domestic-reforms/>.

Mancini, Mark. "The Time Peter the Great Declared War on Facial Hair." *Mental Floss*. Mental Floss, Inc., 29 Mar. 2014. Web. 2 May 2017. <http://mentalfloss.com/article/55772/time-peter-great-declared-war-facial-hair>.

Christina. "Peter the Great Trendsetter: National Change through Fashion." *Daydream Tourist*. WordPress, 8 Sept. 2015. Web. 2 May 2017. <https://daydreamtourist.com/2015/09/08/peter-the-great-fashion/>.

Editors, Reddit. "Does anybody know the value of a Ruble in 1860?" *Reddit*. Reddit, Inc., 2015. Web. 2 May 2017. <https://www.reddit.com/r/AskHistorians/comments/2o7vcl/does_anybody_know_the_value_o f_a_ruble_in_1860/>.

Editors, Hermitage Amsterdam. "St Petersburg & Russia." *Hermitage Amsterdam*. Hermitage Amsterdam, 2015. Web. 2 May 2017. <http://www.hermitage.nl/en/st-petersburg_en_rusland/nederland_rusland_en_st-petersburg/de_huisjes_van_tsaar_peter.htm>.

Editors, RusArt.Net. "Winter Canal." *RusArt.Net*. RusArt.Net, 2016. Web. 2 May 2017. <http://www.rusartnet.com/russia/st-petersburg/architecture/canal/winter-canal>.

Authors, Saint Petersburg . "Menshikov Palace." *Saint Petersburg* . Saint Petersburg.Com, 2016. Web. 2 May 2017. <http://www.saint-petersburg.com/museums/hermitage-museum/menshikov-palace/>.

Wright, Jennifer. "Anna Ivanovna's Ice Palace." *Slate*. The Slate Group, LLC, 6 Dec. 2015. Web. 2 May 2017. <http://www.slate.com/articles/arts/culturebox/2015/11/empress_anna_ivanovna_of_russia_hat ed_love_and_marriage_so_much_that_she.html>.

Editors, Fodors' Travel. "STATE HERMITAGE MUSEUM (GOSUDARSTVENNY ERMITAZH MUZEY)." *Fodors' Travel*. Internet Brands, Inc., 2017. Web. 2 May 2017. <http://www.fodors.com/world/europe/russia/st-petersburg/things-to-do/sights/reviews/state-hermitage-museum-154816>.

Editors, History is Now. "Catherine the Great and her many lovers. Just don't mention the horses…." *History is Now*. History is Now Magazine, 5 Feb. 2015. Web. 3 May 2017. <http://www.historyisnowmagazine.com/blog/2015/1/31/catherine-the-great-and-her-many-lovers-just-dont-mention-the-horses#.WQxXE-WGNPY=>.

Perrottet, Tony. "HORSING AROUND WITH CATHERINE THE GREAT." *TONY'S SECRET CABINET*. Tony Perrottet, 25 Feb. 2008. Web. 3 May 2017. <http://thesmartset.com/article02250801/>.

Maranzani, Barbara. "8 Things You Didn't Know About Catherine the Great." *History in the Headlines*. A&E Television Networks, LLC, 9 July 2012. Web. 3 May 2017. <http://www.history.com/news/8-things-you-didnt-know-about-catherine-the-great>.

Editors, Catherine the Great. "Catherine the Great - Lovers." *Catherine the Great*. Weebly, Inc., 2007. Web. 3 May 2017. <http://katherineandcatherinethegreat.weebly.com/marriage--love.html>.

Wolff, Larry. "'If I Were Younger I Would Make Myself Russian': Voltaire's Encounter With the Czars." *The New York Times*. The New York Times Company, 13 Nov. 1994. Web. 3 May 2017. <http://www.nytimes.com/1994/11/13/books/if-were-younger-would-make-myself-russian-voltaire-s-encounter-with-czars.html?pagewanted=all>.

Osborn, Andrew. "Voltaire and Catherine the Great: a pair of unlikely pen-pals." *The Independent Online*. Associated Newspapers, Ltd., 1 June 2006. Web. 3 May 2017. <http://www.independent.co.uk/news/world/europe/voltaire-and-catherine-the-great-a-pair-of-unlikely-pen-pals-480746.html>.

Authors, The State Hermitage Museum. "The Construction of the Small Hermitage." *The State Hermitage Museum*. The State Hermitage Museum, 2017. Web. 3 May 2017. <http://www.hermitagemuseum.org/wps/portal/hermitage/explore/history/historical-article/1750/Construction of the Small Hermitage/?lng=pl>.

Authors, The State Hermitage Museum. "The Acquisition of J.E. Gotzkowsky's Collection by Catherine II." *The State Hermitage Museum*. The State Hermitage Museum, 2017. Web. 4 May 2017. <https://www.hermitagemuseum.org/wps/portal/hermitage/explore/history/historical-article/1750/Empress Catherine II purchases Johann Ernest Gotzkowskis collection/?lng=>.

Editors, Totally History. "Danaë." *Totally History*. Totally History, Ltd., 25 Nov. 2015. Web. 4 May 2017. <http://totallyhistory.com/danae/>.

Authors, Saint Petersburg . "Explore the Hermitage: An introduction to St. Petersburg's greatest museum." *Saint Petersburg* . Saint Petersburg.Com, 2017. Web. 4 May 2017. <http://www.traceyourdutchroots.com/art/idlers.html>.

Authors, The State Hermitage Museum. "The Great (Old) Hermitage." *The State Hermitage Museum*. The State Hermitage Museum, 2017. Web. 4 May 2017. <https://www.hermitagemuseum.org/wps/portal/hermitage/explore/buildings/locations/building/B30/?lng=en>.

Morris, Roderick Conway. "The Hermitage and Catherine the Great Collector." *The New York Times*. The New York Times Company, 11 July 1998. Web. 4 May 2017.

<http://www.nytimes.com/1998/07/11/style/the-hermitage-and-catherine-the-great-collector.html>.

Editors, Your Dictionary. "Alexander I Facts." *Your Dictionary Biographies*. LoveToKnow Corporation, 2003. Web. 4 May 2017. <http://biography.yourdictionary.com/alexander-i>.

Greenspan, Jesse. "Napoleon's Disastrous Invasion of Russia." *History in the Headlines*. A&E Television Networks, LLC, 22 June 2012. Web. 4 May 2017. <http://www.history.com/news/napoleons-disastrous-invasion-of-russia-200-years-ago>.

Editors, Hermitage Amsterdam. "Alexander, Napoleon & Joséphine, a Story of Friendship, War and Art from the Hermitage." *Hermitage Amsterdam*. Hermitage Amsterdam, 2015. Web. 4 May 2017. <https://www.hermitage.nl/en/tentoonstellingen/alexander_napoleon_josephine/backgroundstory.htm>.

Editors, The State Hermitage Museum. "The General Staff Building." *The State Hermitage Museum*. The State Hermitage Museum, 2017. Web. 4 May 2017. <https://www.hermitagemuseum.org/wps/portal/hermitage/explore/buildings/locations/building/B60/?lng=>.

Editors, UNESCO. "HISTORY OF THE GENERAL STAFF BUILDING." *UNESCO*. UNESCO Organization, 2014. Web. 4 May 2017. <http://www.unesco.org/culture/hermitage/html_eng/hisofgeneralstaff.htm>.

Authors, Saint Petersburg . "General Staff Building." *Saint Petersburg* . Saint Petersburg.Com, 2016. Web. 4 May 2017. <http://www.saint-petersburg.com/museums/hermitage-museum/general-staff-building/>.

Editors, Russiapedia. "Prominent Russians: Nicholas I." *Russiapedia*. Autonomous Nonprofit Organization, 2005. Web. 4 May 2017. <http://russiapedia.rt.com/prominent-russians/the-romanov-dynasty/nicholas-i/>.

Authors, The State Hermitage Museum. "The New Hermitage." *The State Hermitage Museum*. The State Hermitage Museum, 2017. Web. 4 May 2017. <https://www.hermitagemuseum.org/wps/portal/hermitage/explore/buildings/locations/building/B40/?lng=en>.

Authors, The State Hermitage Museum. "The Acquisition of the Barbarigo Gallery Collection." *The State Hermitage Museum*. The State Hermitage Museum, 2017. Web. 4 May 2017. <https://www.hermitagemuseum.org/wps/portal/hermitage/explore/history/historical-article/1850/Purchase of the Cristoforo Barbarigo collection/?lng=>.

Robson, John. "Hermitage Opened – It Happened Today, February 5." *John Robson Online.* John Robson, 5 Feb. 2017. Web. 5 May 2017. <http://www.thejohnrobson.com/hermitage-opened-it-happened-today-february-5/>.

Editors, Presidential Library. "New Hermitage, the first public art museum in Russia, was opened." *Presidential Library.* Yeltsin Presidential Library, 1990. Web. 5 May 2017. <http://www.prlib.ru/en-us/History/Pages/Item.aspx?itemid=419>.

Editors, The Street and the City. "February 5, 1852: Opening of the New Hermitage Museum in Saint Petersburg." *The Street and the City.* WordPress, 5 Feb. 2016. Web. 5 May 2017. <https://thestreetandthecityul.wordpress.com/2016/02/05/february-5-1852-opening-of-the-new-hermitage-museum-in-saint-petersburg/>.

Lynch, Michael. "The Emancipation of the Russian Serfs, 1861: A Charter of Freedom or an Act of Betrayal?" *History Today.* History Today, Ltd., Dec. 2003. Web. 5 May 2017. <http://www.historytoday.com/michael-lynch/emancipation-russian-serfs-1861-charter-freedom-or-act-betrayal>.

Editors, The Virtual Russian Museum. "Portrait of Alexander II." *The Virtual Russian Museum.* The Virtual Russian Museum - St. Petersburg, 2014. Web. 5 May 2017. <http://rusmuseumvrm.ru/data/collections/painting/19_20/botman_ei_portret_aleksandra_ii_18 56_zhb_1942/index.php?lang=en>.

Authors, The State Hermitage Museum. "The Acquisition of the Marquis Gian Pietro Campana Collection." *The State Hermitage Museum.* The State Hermitage Museum, 2017. Web. 5 May 2017. <https://www.hermitagemuseum.org/wps/portal/hermitage/explore/history/historical-article/1850/Campana collection/?lng=>.

Authors, The State Hermitage Museum. "The Purchase of Raphael's "Conestabile Madonna"." *The State Hermitage Museum.* The State Hermitage Museum, 2017. Web. 5 May 2017. <https://www.hermitagemuseum.org/wps/portal/hermitage/explore/history/historical-article/1850/Madonna by Raphael/?lng=en>.

Authors, The State Hermitage Museum. "The Acquisition of the A.P.Basilewski Collection." *The State Hermitage Museum.* The State Hermitage Museum, 2017. Web. 5 May 2017. <https://www.hermitagemuseum.org/wps/portal/hermitage/explore/history/historical-article/1850/Basilevsky collection/?lng=en>.

Authors, The State Hermitage Museum. "The Acquisition of Leonardo da Vinci's "Madonna and Child" (the "Benois Madonna")." *The State Hermitage Museum.* The State Hermitage Museum, 2017. Web. 5 May 2017.

<https://www.hermitagemuseum.org/wps/portal/hermitage/explore/history/historical-article/1900/Purchase of Leonardo da Vincis Madonna with a Flower %28Benois Madonna%29/?lng=>.

Gruver, Rebecca. "What was a Franc worth in today's terms during the time Les Miserables took place?" *Quora*. Quora, Inc., 30 Jan. 2013. Web. 5 May 2017. <https://www.quora.com/What-was-a-Franc-worth-in-todays-terms-during-the-time-Les-Miserables-took-place>.

Authors, The State Hermitage Museum. "A Hospital in the Winter Palace. 1915-1917." *The State Hermitage Museum*. The State Hermitage Museum, 2017. Web. 5 May 2017. <http://www.hermitagemuseum.org/wps/portal/hermitage/what-s-on/temp_exh/1999_2013/hm4_1_127/?lng=en>.

Editors, History Channel. "February Revolution begins in Russia." *History Channel*. A&E Television Networks, LLC, 8 Mar. 2015. Web. 5 May 2017. <http://www.history.com/this-day-in-history/february-revolution-begins-in-russia>.

Authors, The State Hermitage Museum. "Art Works - Bean King." *The State Hermitage Museum*. The State Hermitage Museum, 2017. Web. 5 May 2017. <https://www.hermitagemuseum.org/wps/portal/hermitage/digital-collection/01. Paintings/48341/?lng=>.

Authors, The State Hermitage Museum. "Art Works - Angel of the Death." *The State Hermitage Museum*. The State Hermitage Museum, 2017. Web. 5 May 2017. <http://www.hermitagemuseum.org/wps/portal/hermitage/digital-collection/01. Paintings/37074/?lng=ja>.

Authors, Heresy & Beauty. "The Angel of the Death." *Heresy & Beauty*. WordPress, 1 Apr. 2010. Web. 5 May 2017. <https://heresyandbeauty.wordpress.com/2010/04/01/the-angel-of-the-death/>.

Editors, History Channel. "USSR established." *History Channel*. A&E Television Networks, LLC, 30 Dec. 2014. Web. 5 May 2017. <http://www.history.com/this-day-in-history/ussr-established>.

Hingley, Ronald Francis. "Joseph Stalin." *Encyclopedia Britannica*. Encyclopedia Britannica, Inc., 2012. Web. 5 May 2017. <https://www.britannica.com/biography/Joseph-Stalin>.

Editors, Calouste Gulbenkian Museum. "The Collector - Calouste Sarkis Gulbenkian." *Calouste Gulbenkian Museum*. Calouste Gulbenkian Museum, 2014. Web. 5 May 2017. <https://gulbenkian.pt/museu/en/the-founders-collection/the-collector/>.

Editors, National Geographic. "Top 10 Museums and Galleries." *National Geographic News*. National Geographic Society, 20 Sept. 2012. Web. 5 May 2017. <http://www.nationalgeographic.com/travel/top-10/museum-galleries/>.

Krasnov, Oleg. "Moscow's and St. Petersburg's top 5 most visited museums revealed." *Russia Beyond the Headlines*. Autonomous Nonprofit Organization, 18 June 2016. Web. 5 May 2017. <https://rbth.com/arts/2016/06/18/moscows-and-st-petersburgs-top-5-most-visited-museums-revealed_604065>.

Rounding, Virginia. *Catherine the Great: Love, Sex, and Power*. 1st ed. N.p.: St. Martin's Griffin, 2008. Print.

Neal, Larry. *A Concise History of International Finance: From Babylon to Bernanke (New Approaches to Economic and Social History)*. N.p.: Cambridge U Press, 2015. Print. New Approaches to Economic and Social History.

Giebelhausen, Michaela. *The Architecture of the Museum: Symbolic Structures, Urban Contexts (Critical Perspectives in Art History)*. N.p.: Manchester U Press, 2003. Print. Critical Perspectives in Art History.

Massie, Robert K. *Peter the Great: His Life and World*. N.p.: Random House Trade, 1981. Print.

Denton, C. S. *Absolute Power: The Real Lives of Europe's Most Infamous Rulers*. N.p.: Eagle Editions, 2006. Print.

Lang, Se?n. *European History For Dummies*. 2nd ed. N.p.: For Dummies, 2011. Print.

Free Books by Charles River Editors

We have brand new titles available for free most days of the week. To see which of our titles are currently free, click on this link.

Discounted Books by Charles River Editors

We have titles at a discount price of just 99 cents everyday. To see which of our titles are currently 99 cents, click on this link.

Made in the USA
San Bernardino, CA
13 June 2018